Natural Disasters

Tsunamis

Louise Park

Smart Apple Media

This edition first published in 2008 in the United States of America by Smart Apple Media.

Smart Apple Media
2140 Howard Drive West
North Mankato, Minnesota 56003

First published in 2007 by
MACMILLAN EDUCATION AUSTRALIA PTY LTD
627 Chapel Street, South Yarra, Australia 3141

Visit our Web site at www.macmillan.com.au or go directly to www.macmillanlibrary.com.au

Associated companies and representatives throughout the world.

Library of Congress Cataloging-in-Publication Data

Park, Louise, 1961-
    Tsunamis / by Louise Park.
    p. cm. – (Natural disasters)
    Includes index.
    ISBN 978-1-59920-115-3
    1. Tsunamis–Juvenile literature. I. Title.

    GC221.5.P36 2007
    363.34'94–dc22

2007004661

Edited by Sam Munday and Erin Richards
Text and cover design by Ivan Finnegan, iF design
Page layout by Ivan Finnegan, iF design
Photo research by Jes Senbergs
Illustrations by Andy Craig and Nives Porcellato, pp. 7, 10, 11, 13, 21
Maps by designscope, pp. 6, 8, 14, 18, 20, 26

Printed in U.S.

Acknowledgements
The author and the publisher are grateful to the following for permission to reproduce copyright material:
Front cover photograph: tsunami wave engulfs Phuket's Chedi resort restaurant, December 2004, courtesy of AAP/AFP Photo.

Background textures courtesy of Ivan Finnegan, iF design.

AAP/AFP Photo, pp. 1, 8, 23; AAP/AP Photo/Ronen Zilberman, p. 24; AAP/EPA/STR, p. 4; Ausaid/ Robin Davies, p. 9; FairfaxPhotos/ John Russell, p. 5; FairfaxPhotos/Angela Wylie, p. 22; Richard Farmer, p. 15; Kenneth Hamm/Photo Japan, p. 14; David Hardy/Science Photo Library, p. 18; Palani Mohan/Getty Images, p. 28; NDGS, pp. 26, 27; Newspix, p. 29; Popperfoto/Alamy, p. 16; Reuters/Picture Media, p. 17; Tom Van Sant/Geosphere Project, Santa Monica/Science Photo Library, p. 25; USGS, p. 19; Zephyr/Science Photo Library, p. 12.

Contents

GLOSSARY WORDS
When a word is printed in **bold**, you can look up its meaning in the glossary on page 31.

Natural disasters

Natural disasters are events that occur naturally. They are not caused by human action. They can happen all over the world at any time. When natural disasters occur in populated areas, they can result in death, injury, and damage to property.

Types of natural disasters

There are many types of natural disasters, such as tornadoes, wildfires, droughts, and earthquakes. Each type occurs for very different reasons and affects Earth in different ways. Although they are different, they all create chaos and bring **devastation** and destruction with them wherever they strike.

The 2004 Indian Ocean tsunami destroyed holiday bungalows at this beach resort in Thailand.

Tsunamis

The oceans are an important part of our planet. They cover more than 70 percent of Earth's surface. However, when there is an **undersea disturbance**, these oceans can suddenly become very dangerous. Tsunami waves are powerful walls of water. These waves can move across the open ocean at speeds of up to 560 miles (900 km) an hour—as fast as a plane. When they hit the coastline, these enormous waves can reach up to 100 feet (30 m) in height.

DID YOU KNOW?
A tsunami is not just one wave. It is a series of huge waves that happens after undersea earthquakes, volcano eruptions, and other sea disturbances occur. Most tsunamis occur in the Pacific region but they can happen in every ocean and sea.

Tsunami waves approaching shore can reach incredible heights.

What is a tsunami?

A tsunami is a series of huge waves. These huge waves occur when there is a massive disturbance under the sea. Sometimes tsunamis are mistakenly called **tidal waves**. This is because they look like an onrushing **tide** as they approach land. However, tsunamis do not occur as a result of tides, so this term is not accurate.

Tsunami waves travel out in all directions from the point of the undersea disturbance. As these big waves approach land, they grow much taller. This is because shallow waters near land cause the water from a tsunami to pile up. This creates an enormous wall of water that smashes onto the coast.

DID YOU KNOW?
The name tsunami comes from the Japanese language. It means "harbor wave."

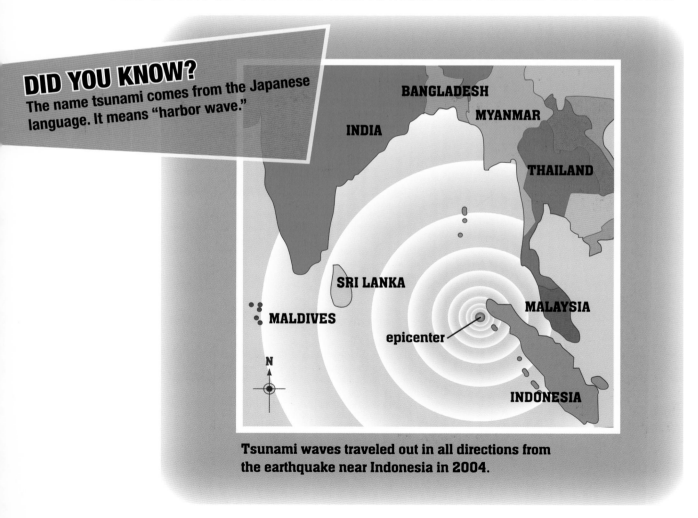

Tsunami waves traveled out in all directions from the earthquake near Indonesia in 2004.

Tsunami waves

Tsunamis waves are not the same as other waves. They do not look like giant versions of normal waves and they are formed differently. Tsunamis do not curl and swell like waves that surfers might ride. Tsunamis look like an endless onrushing tide, which is why they flood coastal areas. Normal waves are usually formed by:

- wind blowing across the surface of the water

- incoming and outgoing tides

Tsunamis are created by undersea disturbances and are huge movements of water. They begin in deep sea and travel at very high speeds for long distances. Tsunamis can cause damage thousands of miles from where they began. It may be hours before the waves strike land. Tsunami waves lose very little energy as they travel.

Think about it

Because a tsunami is a series of waves, the first wave may not be the largest or the most dangerous. The worst damage might come later, long after the first wave has struck.

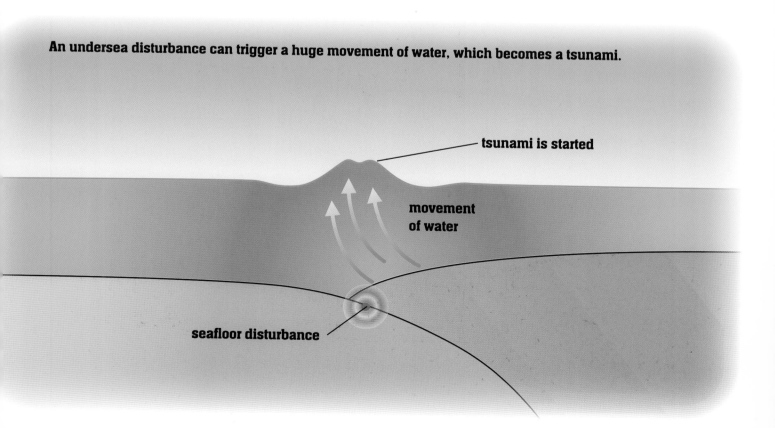

An undersea disturbance can trigger a huge movement of water, which becomes a tsunami.

tsunami is started

movement of water

seafloor disturbance

DISASTER FILE
Indian Ocean

WHAT	The worst tsunami ever recorded
WHERE	Off the coast of Sumatra, Indonesia
WHEN	December 26, 2004
WAVE HEIGHTS	Up to 100 feet (30 m)

On December 26, 2004, the largest earthquake in 40 years took place in the Indian Ocean. The earthquake triggered the deadliest tsunami in world history. It was so powerful that the waves caused devastation on the coast of Africa and were even detected on the east coast of the United States. Eleven countries bordering the Indian Ocean were affected. The tsunami damaged entire cities, ruined farmland, and devastated fishing stocks.

A strong earthquake lasting 20 seconds or more near the coast can generate a tsunami. This undersea earthquake lasted for close to 10 minutes. It caused the entire planet to briefly vibrate. The tsunami it created killed more than 283,100 people.

This is what happened at a resort in Thailand when the tsunami hit.

Why did it happen?

Earth's **crust** is made of **tectonic plates**. These plates are always moving and bumping or rubbing together. Most earthquakes occur along the boundaries of tectonic plates. There is a complex structure of boundaries near Sumatra in Indonesia. On December 26, 2004, a rupture occurred at a boundary when one tectonic plate slipped underneath another.

Counting the cost

The damage and destruction from this tsunami was extensive. Apart from the massive human death toll, it has been estimated that another 1,126,900 people lost their homes. Damage to rain forests, coral reefs, land, and **vegetation** was also extensive. Salt water destroyed freshwater areas and polluted freshwater supplies. This led to people losing their livelihoods and caused shortages of food and water.

The tsunami devastated the coastline of Sri Lanka.

How tsunamis are created

Tsunamis are created when there is a disturbance in the seafloor that increases the sea level suddenly. The higher sea levels are like massive shelves of water that move toward land. The rise in sea level and the pressure of the sea behind it creates enormous force.

Tsunami waves begin in deep water. From where the undersea disturbance occurs, waves travel outward in all directions, just like the ripples caused by throwing a rock into a pond. From one disturbance, the tsunami that is created can involve a number of waves. These are known as wave trains. These waves can be hours behind each other.

Think about it

The Indian Ocean tsunami in 2004 was caused by the India Plate moving sideways and under the Burma Plate. This displaced an enormous volume of water.

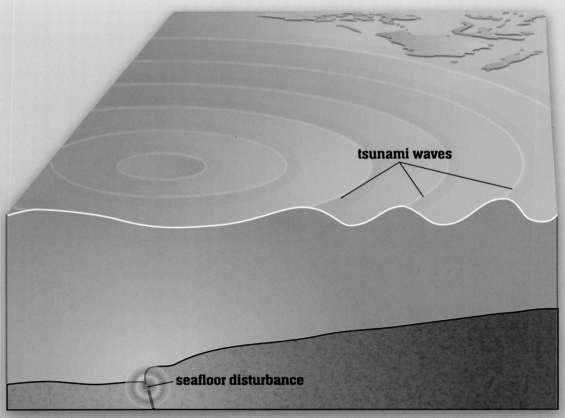

tsunami waves

seafloor disturbance

Wave trains travel across the ocean at enormous speeds.

How a tsunami builds up

Tsunamis that begin in deep water travel at a fast speed. The deeper the water, the faster they travel. In deep water, these waves are very small and can even go undetected. As the tsunami moves into shallow waters near the coast, the waves build up. When this happens, a great wall of water pushes over the coastline with tremendous force.

A tsunami wave can become enormous very quickly as it hits the shallow waters near the coast. When other waves follow and join it, this makes the tsunami even higher and stronger.

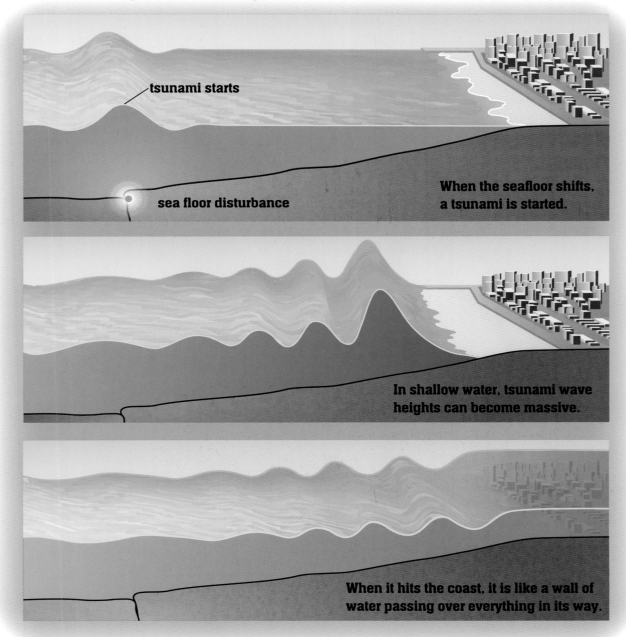

tsunami starts

sea floor disturbance

When the seafloor shifts, a tsunami is started.

In shallow water, tsunami wave heights can become massive.

When it hits the coast, it is like a wall of water passing over everything in its way.

Common causes of tsunamis

Tsunamis begin when a huge volume of water is moved suddenly. This rapid movement happens as the result of the seafloor moving up or down very quickly. The most common cause of seafloor movement is an earthquake.

Earthquakes

Most tsunamis are caused by earthquakes. However, not every earthquake produces a tsunami. For an earthquake to generate a tsunami, it generally needs to measure over 6.0 on the **Richter scale**.

Most earthquakes occur along the boundaries of tectonic plates. Different boundaries cause different types of earthquakes and plate movement. For a tsunami to occur, there usually needs to be some vertical movement or sliding movement.

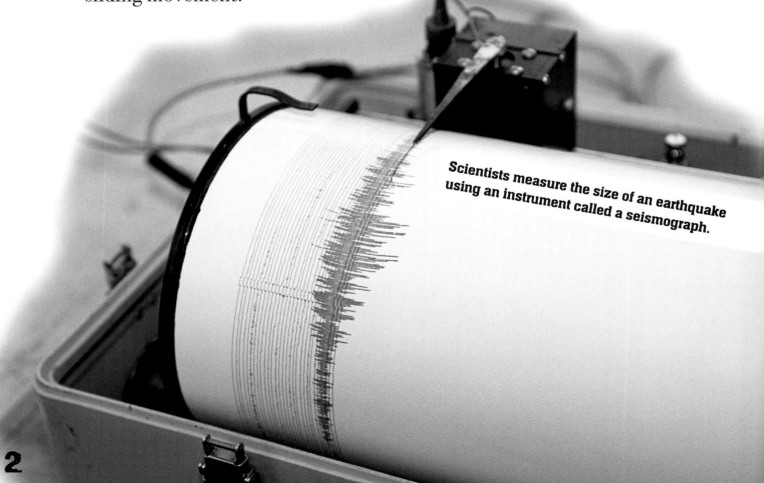

Scientists measure the size of an earthquake using an instrument called a seismograph.

Vertical movement

Very strong earthquakes happen at the site of **convergent boundaries**. Convergent boundaries occur when one plate slides over the top of another. The lower plate gets pushed down into the **mantle** and starts to melt. This vertical movement displaces huge amounts of water. This wall of water is the beginning of a tsunami.

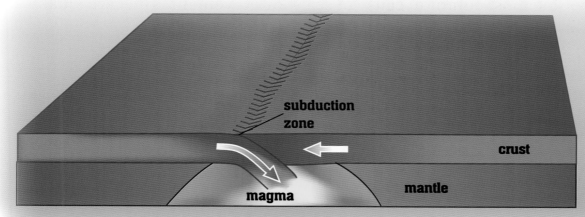

At convergent boundaries, the zone where the two plates meet is called the subduction zone.

Sliding movement

Transform boundaries slide past each other. When this happens, the buildup and release of strain as the plates slide produces earthquakes. Sometimes, the plates cause so much stress that they break and create gaps known as faults. These gaps cannot be closed. As the plates along these fault lines continue to grind past each other, weak rock crumbles. Stronger rocks just keep pushing and pulling against each other, releasing enormous amounts of energy.

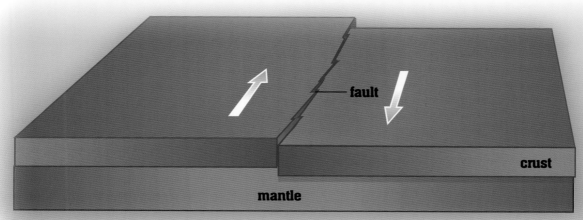

At transform boundaries, plates grind past each other.

DISASTER FILE
Sanriku, Japan

WHAT	The most devastating tsunami in Japanese history
WHERE	Off the coast of Sanriku, Japan
WHEN	June 15, 1896
WAVE HEIGHTS	Up to 82 feet (25 m)

On June 15, 1896, thousands of people gathered on the Sanriku coast to celebrate a holiday. Most did not feel the beginnings of the earthquake that had begun **offshore**. After an initial weak shock, five minutes of extremely slow shaking followed. Then the sea withdrew abruptly. About 30 minutes after the earthquake, a huge tsunami hit the Sanriku coast.

The coastline of Sanriku was devastated by the tsunami.

Think about it
This tsunami has fascinated scientists for years. Scientists know that tsunamis are generated by undersea earthquakes. What is intriguing about this tsunami is its size. It was much larger than scientists expected, based on the size of the earthquake that caused it.

Why did it happen?

This tsunami was caused by an undersea earthquake. Research indicates that the earthquake was very close to the Japan Trench. This trench is part of the Pacific Ring of Fire. It was created when seafloor spreading occurred, building an underwater mountain.

Counting the cost

The tsunami that hit Sanriku reached huge heights. When it struck, it instantly swept away all the houses and people in its path. The wave hit over 170 miles (275 km) of coastline and wiped out more than 13,000 homes. It destroyed over 7,000 fishing boats and claimed 28,000 lives. Ten and a half hours later, the wave hit the shores of San Francisco, over 5,000 miles (8,000 km) away. This tsunami also caused damage as far off as Hawaii.

Many coastal towns in Japan are now protected by tsunami walls.

Other causes of tsunamis

Landslides and volcanic eruptions can both cause tsunamis to begin.

Landslides

Sometimes tsunami waves can be generated from rockfalls and icefalls or sudden undersea landslides. Generally, the energy of tsunami waves generated from landslides or rockfalls is less than that generated from earthquakes. But sometimes the landslides are so large that huge tsunami waves can be created.

One of the largest tsunami waves ever observed was caused by a rockslide. It was the result of an earthquake that occurred in Alaska in 1958. Massive amounts of rock tumbled into Lituya Bay. This generated a wave which reached a height of more than 1,700 feet (520 m).

DID YOU KNOW?
In 1963, nearly 2,000 people were killed when a landslide hit the reservoir behind Vajont Dam in Northern Italy. The landslide triggered a tsunami that went over the top of the dam and into the valley below.

Whole villages were swept away by the tsunami at Vajont Dam.

Volcanoes

Tsunamis can also begin as a result of a volcanic eruption. If an underwater volcano erupts, it can affect the water in three ways:

- massive flows of **debris** and ash travel down, suddenly pushing water outward

- a release of hot **lava** may heat the surrounding water quickly

- the top of an underwater volcano may collapse inward, creating a crater that water can suddenly pour into

Tsunamis generated from volcanic activity are not as common as tsunamis generated by earthquakes. However, when they do occur, they can cause significant damage to coastal areas.

Think about it

The most destructive volcanic eruption in Japan produced a tsunami. In 1792, the Unzen volcano erupted. It produced a landslide from its eastern side that crashed into the Ariake Sea. This created a tsunami that killed about 14,500 people.

An underwater volcanic eruption can move enough water to create a tsunami.

DISASTER FILE
Krakatoa, Indonesia

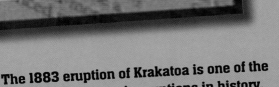

WHAT	The worst tsunamis ever generated from a volcanic eruption
WHERE	Krakatoa, Indonesia
WHEN	August 1883
WAVE HEIGHTS	Up to 130 feet (40 m)

When the volcano Krakatoa erupted in August 1883, it created some of the biggest and most destructive tsunamis ever recorded. Its final eruptions during that year involved four enormous explosions. These explosions were so loud and violent that they were heard over 2,000 miles (3,220 km) away, in Australia. Ash was propelled as high as 50 miles (80 km). Each of these massive explosions generated its own set of deadly tsunamis.

The 1883 eruption of Krakatoa is one of the most violent volcanic eruptions in history.

Think about it

This Krakatoa eruption was so severe that it disturbed the world's weather pattern for nearly five years. The atmosphere was filled with so much volcanic dust that it blocked a certain amount of sunlight from reaching Earth. Temperatures all around the world were lowered and did not return to normal until 1888.

Why did it happen?

It is believed that gigantic pyroclastic flows from each explosion entered the sea. Pyroclastic flows are mixtures of hot, dry rock and hot gases that move at high speeds. Some of these flows traveled 25 miles (40 km) across the water to the coast of Sumatra. Undersea pyroclastic flows are also believed to have occurred. All of this material entering the sea displaced enormous amounts of water.

Counting the cost

The lethal tsunamis generated from these explosions destroyed entire towns. Waves reaching up to 130 feet (40 m) high hit the shores and left no survivors on the island of Sebesi. The official death toll was recorded at 36,417. Many villages, towns, and settlements were completely wiped out along the Sunda Strait on the islands of Java and Sumatra.

Pyroclastic flows are sometimes known as burning clouds.

Where tsunamis happen

Most tsunamis happen in the Pacific Ocean. This is because the Pacific Ocean has more earthquakes and volcanic activity than anywhere else. The Pacific Ocean is surrounded by the Ring of Fire. The Ring of Fire is a highly active volcano and earthquake zone. Although tsunamis begin in the ocean, their destruction occurs when the waves hit land. Tsunamis occur in coastal regions with waves frequently hitting islands.

DID YOU KNOW?

It is not just the tsunami waves that can do dama
Tsunamis push large amounts of water onto the s
above the regular sea level. This is called a run-up
Run-ups can cause tremendous inland damage to
property, vegetation, soil, and freshwater supplies

The Ring of Fire circles the Pacific Ocean from Alaska, the west coasts of North and South America, and the east coast of Asia.

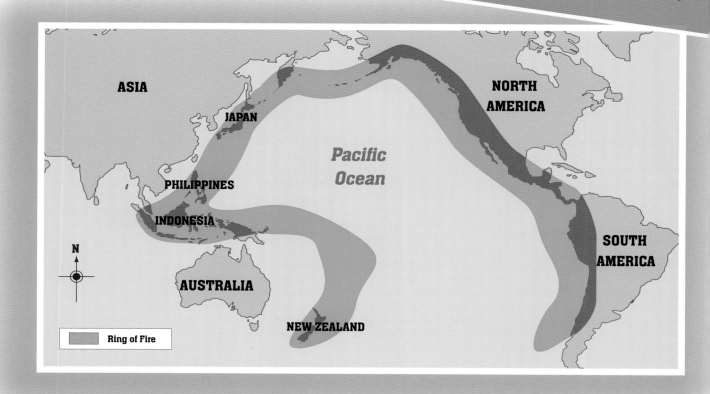

ASIA

JAPAN

PHILIPPINES

INDONESIA

N

AUSTRALIA

NEW ZEALAND

Pacific Ocean

NORTH AMERICA

SOUTH AMERICA

Ring of Fire

How do tsunamis travel?

Tsunamis are made of a series of extremely long waves. These waves can sometimes be more than 125 miles (200 km) long. When a tsunami is created from an earthquake over a large area, its wave lengths are also large. Tsunamis caused by landslides tend to have shorter wave lengths. The time between waves in a tsunami can range from 5 to 90 minutes apart.

The wave train travels outward on the surface of the ocean in all directions. In the deep ocean, the height of the tsunami might only be a few feet (about 1m). This makes them barely visible and hard to detect. However, these walls of water can travel at speeds of up to 600 miles (970 km) an hour. The deeper the water, the greater the speed of the tsunami.

Think about it

The tsunami generated by an earthquake in Chile in 1960 wasted no time moving across the ocean. It reached Japan, more than 10,440 miles (16,800 km) away, in less than 24 hours.

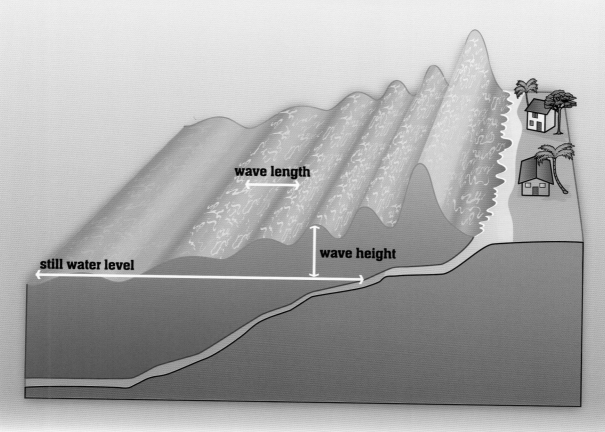

Tsunami waves start deep in the sea and build up as they approach the shore.

wave length

wave height

still water level

When tsunamis hit

When tsunamis hit the coastline, they can cause great loss of life and property damage. The power of these walls of water can be enormous. Tsunamis are capable of completely destroying buildings. They can lift cars and boats and hurl them great distances. One tsunami can easily devastate entire coastal villages and beaches.

Tsunamis can also cause long-term damage to the environment. Saltwater tsunamis can destroy crops and ruin the soil. The damage done can take years to be repaired. They can destroy all of an area's vegetation and pollute the water supplies.

DID YOU KNOW?
In 1998, three giant tsunami waves hit the shores of Papua New Guinea. This wave train completely destroyed villages between Aitape and Seai. Over 2,000 people were drowned and over 10,000 were left homeless.

Three successive waves caused massive destruction to the villages of Papua New Guinea.

Signs of a tsunami approaching

Sometimes there are signs that a tsunami is on its way. Often, just before a tsunami hits, the ocean can be sucked away from the beach. People can be intrigued by this phenomenon and may flock to the beach to look at it. This is the worst thing to do. When the tsunami arrives, it does so as a wall of water, moving at a high speed. The people on the beach could then become the first victims of the tsunami.

Other signs include:

- feeling the tremors of an earthquake

- the water becoming unusually hot

- hearing a roaring noise like a plane overhead

The sea disappeared from this beach before the Indian Ocean tsunami rushed in.

Forecasting tsunamis

Tsunamis cannot be prevented, but warning systems and forecasting tools can minimize the damage caused. All around the world, information and data is collected on earthquake and volcanic activity. When earthquakes or volcanic eruptions capable of producing tsunamis are recorded, warnings are issued. Scientists are constantly working on new and more accurate methods of gathering and analyzing this data.

Pacific Tsunami Warning System

Most tsunamis occur in the Pacific Ocean because of the Ring of Fire. The Pacific Tsunami Warning System was developed to protect people at risk in this area. This group monitors tidal and **seismic activity** throughout the Pacific Basin. When tsunamis are predicted, this information is passed on to the Pacific Warning Center in Hawaii. Scientists here can locate and predict where the tsunamis are headed. They can then warn people who are threatened by these waves.

Scientists study Earth's seismic activity so they can predict when tsunamis might occur.

Measuring the waves

Measuring the height of tsunami waves is very difficult during the event. The most common method is called "run-up" measurements. Run-up heights are measured by looking at the distance and extent of vegetation killed by salt. Run-ups also look at the debris that is left once the wave has receded.

Radar satellites that orbit Earth are being used more and more to measure waves. The height of the waves that hit Sumatra in December 2004 was measured using these satellites. This technology allows scientists to make deep-sea surveys from space. Researchers believe these satellites will greatly improve the forecasting of tsunamis. Monitoring and mapping the ocean floor from space is one way to observe dangerous changes.

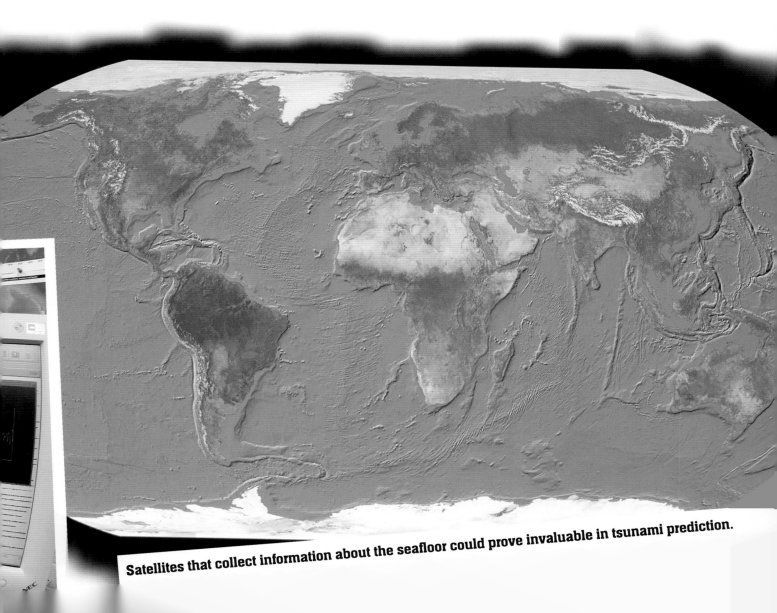

Satellites that collect information about the seafloor could prove invaluable in tsunami prediction.

DISASTER FILE
The Aleutian Islands

WHAT	The tsunami responsible for the Pacific Tsunami Warning System
WHERE	Aleutian Islands off Alaska
WHEN	April 1946
WAVE HEIGHTS	Up to 100 feet (30 m)

On April 1, 1946, a strong earthquake struck the Aleutian Islands. This generated a series of deadly tsunami waves. As a direct result of these tsunamis, a warning system was developed. This system is now known as the Pacific Tsunami Warning System.

The earthquake generated some of the most destructive Pacific-wide tsunamis ever recorded. It began with an enormous tsunami smashing onto the coast of Scotch Cap on Unimak Island. Tsunami waves over 100 feet (30 m) high completely destroyed the newly-built lighthouse on Scotch Cap, drowning its crew.

With no lighthouse and crew, warning messages could not be sent out to other places at risk. As a result, less than five hours later, the Hawaiian Islands were caught completely unaware when the first of several tsunamis struck.

Before the tsunami, the Scotch Cap lighthouse stood 40 feet (12 m) above sea level.

Why did it happen?

The earthquake that struck the Aleutian Islands caused a large portion of seafloor to lift up. This piece of seafloor lifted up along the fault where the quake occurred. This caused the Pacific-wide tsunami.

Counting the cost

Tsunamis wreaked havoc along the coastline of the Hawaiian Islands. The area most affected was the town of Hilo, Hawaii. Hilo was pounded by a series of six or seven large tsunami waves arriving at 15–20 minute intervals. The waves smashed their way through the city's waterfront, destroying everything in their path and killing 159 people. The effects of the tsunamis were felt across the west coast of the U.S. Waves also reached Chile and French Polynesia.

The Scotch Cap lighthouse was completely destroyed by the massive tsunami.

Disaster relief

Once the tsunami is over, it is time to assess the extent of damage and destruction. The first step is to rescue any survivors. Tsunamis can leave people stranded in all sorts of strange places. People have been found floating on debris, stranded up in trees, and anywhere else that may have been high enough to give some safety from the water. Areas are set up where relief can be provided to victims. People who have suffered the effects of a tsunami may need medical attention, clothing, shelter, food, and fresh water.

After relief efforts have been established, workers can assess the damage and begin cleaning up. Rebuilding and rehabilitation can then begin. Rehabilitation frequently includes soil restoration and the return of freshwater supplies that may have been ruined by the effects of salt water. This can place strain on the economy of the country and on its government. Sometimes, extensive damage attracts aid from other countries that wish to help.

Rescue workers search the debris for survivors after the Indian Ocean tsunami.

Living with tsunamis

Many governments and organizations around the world pull together after a disaster like a tsunami. After the initial emergency response has taken place, the hard work begins. Medium-term aid manages disease, loss of shelter, and loss of income. Long-term aid can last from several months to several years. It is needed to rebuild cities and reconstruct lives.

Ruined soil and vegetation can take years to repair. This not only affects food supplies but the local economy as well. Countries in the developing world are particularly at risk of famine. After the tsunami that hit Sumatra in 2004, a huge amount of money and resources were raised. Australia alone donated over $240 million to various Sumatra 2004 aid groups. This money helps support countries as they rebuild and recover.

Cricketers from many different nations took part in a charity match to raise money for Sumatra tsunami victims.

DISASTER FILES AT A GLANCE

The four tsunamis profiled in this book are famous for different reasons. This graph compares the size and impact of the tsunamis.

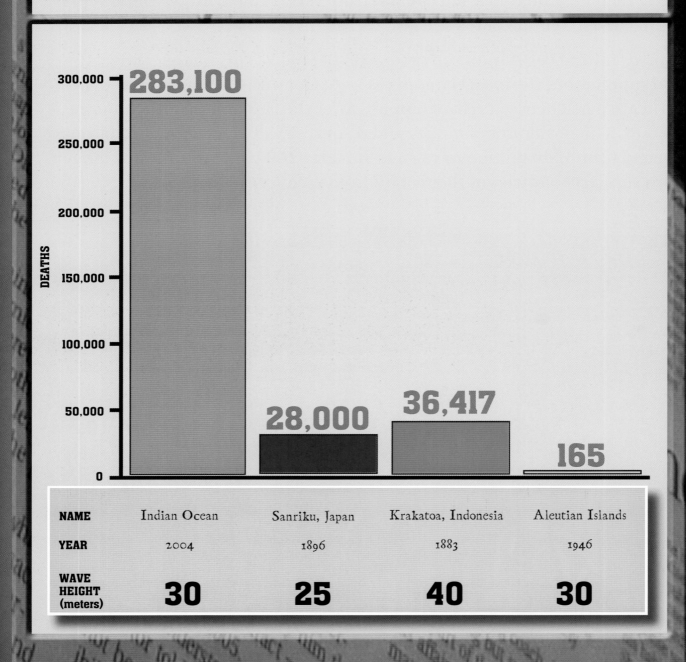

DEATHS

- 283,100
- 28,000
- 36,417
- 165

NAME	Indian Ocean	Sanriku, Japan	Krakatoa, Indonesia	Aleutian Islands
YEAR	2004	1896	1883	1946
WAVE HEIGHT (meters)	30	25	40	30

Glossary

convergent boundaries	where tectonic plates move toward each other
crust	the hard surface layer of Earth
debris	the remains of things that have been broken or destroyed
devastation	severe damage or destruction
lava	hot, liquid rock that has erupted from a volcano
mantle	layer of hot rock beneath Earth's crust
offshore	located a distance from the shore
Richter scale	grading system used to measure the size of earthquakes
seismic activity	the shaking and vibrations inside Earth
tectonic plates	large plates of rock that make up Earth's crust
tidal waves	the swell or crest of surface ocean water, created by the tides
tide	the movement of the sea toward and away from land, caused by the gravitational pull of the Moon
transform boundaries	where tectonic plates slide past each other
undersea disturbance	disturbance in the seafloor, such as an earthquake
vegetation	the plants of an area

Index